GW00789337

Before reading this book, the reader

· two or more letters can represent on

· the spellings ‹ee› ‹e› ‹ea› ‹y› can repr

This book introduces:

· the spellings ‹ee› ‹e› ‹ea› ‹y› for the sound 'ee'
· text at 2 syllable level

High-frequency words:

were, are, said, can't, you, was, family

Vocabulary:

reach   –   to go all the way and arrive somewhere
heap   –   a pile
channel –   a way for water to flow along

Talk about the story:

Dad takes the kids to the beach.
The kids play on a heap of sand
but this heap of sand is not what
it seems to be...

Reading Practice

Practise blending these sounds into words:

ee	e
see	be
free	me
green	he
three	we
street	she

ea	y
seat	jelly
meal	happy
clean	lucky
speak	funny
cream	carry

The Heap of Sand

Dan and Liz went to the beach.

Dan's dad fell asleep. The kids
were happy to be on the beach.

Dan jumped on a heap of sand.

"Get off me!" screamed the heap

of sand. "I am a sea dragon!"

"Sea dragons are not real," said Dan.

"I am real. I live in the sea, but I can't reach it," wept the sea dragon.

"Let me see," said Liz, "let's dig
a channel so that you can swim
back into the deep sea."

4

The kids dug a channel. The sea
dragon swam into the deep sea.
He was happy to see his family.

Then Dad got up. "That's funny,"
he said, "I have just seen three
sea dragons! I must be dreaming!"

Questions for discussion:

- Why was the sea dragon stuck on the beach?

- Why did he need to go back into the sea?

- What do you think the kids said when Dad said, "I must be dreaming!"

Reading game with the sound 'ee'

Play as pelmanism or use for reading practice. Enlarge and photocopy the page twice on two different colours of card. Cut the cards up to play.
Ensure the players sound out the words.

deep	we	sea
jolly	free	begin
team	body	need
she	teach	sunny
sheep	belong	treat